# DEAR DAUGHTER

# DEAR DAUGHTER

By

Samantha Mineroff

ISBN: 979-8-9907612-0-9 (paperback)
ISBN: 979-8-9907612-1-6 (hardcover)

*For those who are healing.*

# Table of Contents

# Apologies

Dear Daughter,
My pain—
       My guilt—
This is not your weight to carry.

And you've had to travel a long, lonely way with
a mountain
on your back.

Please, let me take some of that weight away for
you now.

Dear Daughter,
somber symphonies
        play in the background of this gentle,
        curious mind, one that went from naive
to haunted, from open to
guarded.

The cello is in the hands of my last lover, the
violin playing, betraying blood
the bass the child I once was, trying to survive.

All the while she conducts, wondering if the
tempo will change out of her
control, but knowing well that the music
controls her
until she
finally,
puts it all to
rest.

Dear daughter,
Nostalgia runs through my veins like the wine
from last night, echoing and pulsing.
Was it better then because it was new and ripe?
Is it better now because we've aged and
colored?
I would drown myself in it, if only it didn't take
away light in the next day,
    my brain a buzzing reminder that
    sweetness turns sour.

Maybe one day I can sip with pleasure and not
fear
the next morning.

But for now, I reach
for warmth by candlelight and rain, their
duality a timeless hug that keeps me afloat.

Dear Daughter,
Not only did you not deserve what happened to
you—
        you didn't deserve the aftermath of what
        happened to me too.
Just because I never
        Fully healed—doesn't mean you can't.

In fact—
Your healing,
it poses a
        threat
to me.
If I acknowledge your truth, then I'd have to
believe in mine,
too.

Dearest daughter,
Here I am again, guilt tripped by familiar roots
that extend for you to get your nutrients,
your needs met.
      I'm left, marked and scratched
wounds reopened like an old text book
everyone refused—or forgot—to read.

I grasp at what I can, offer the last shell of me
      the bags under my eyes like tree rings
      the history—dark and
      deep
      and heavy.

There's no more water to wring out from these
      exhausted eyes
that have seen things they shouldn't
but they reflected back at you—
in green, gold, and blue—
Growth means letting go of your branches—

Darling Daughter,

You do not have to forgive me.

I didn't know what would happen. To you, to
our shared mother, Earth.
Even if I did, it was more important for me to
raise you

rather than protect Her.
For how could I have gone on without you?

But now, I see,
that I had a choice—to do both. To care,
and to nurture. To raise you, and to heal our
crumbling structure. All I've known is to grasp
at what is around me,
and those things, they aren't always pleasant.
Arrogance, false confidence, the Lie that
everything would be okay.

Now you are carrying the weight of me, and
what so many others, have done—or didn't do.
I am sorry.
And, I love you, more than our shared mother.

Dear daughter,
No, you were not my only daughter. And still,
you were not the only one who felt forgotten.
I rubbed my grief onto you,

      because you, my darling girl, you are *safe.*
You are safer than what I've known, and I will
never come to realize this, until it's too late.
Until you've realized, perhaps, it's better to take
some space.

My daughter,
I was also a daughter.

We are the same. But we are not meant to weigh
another down.
      Just because I am a daughter,
does not mean I shouldn't have been your
mother.

True, I carry with me my own child self,
      A version of me that I rarely like to see.
That's why I keep our family photos hidden
away, in the dark, in the dust. But no matter

how much I try to push her away, she reappears,
in your laugh,
    your smile,
        your innocence.
I am jealous, my darling girl, because you are
everything.

Dear Daughter,

I see you now, a full, grown woman,
a woman I once was—with thick skin, with
determination,
        understanding.
I was once a woman who defied things, and
now I try to define them.
        I measure you, weigh you, calculate your
        best angles. Because your image is *perfect*.

It's all you have, isn't it?

But now, I am here, old and watching over you,
realizing that I should have appreciated more.
The scars, the freckles, the sagging chin.
        I was worried they'd make me look weak,
        unloved.
But who could ever not love you, in all that you
are?

I didn't know there was another way—I didn't
know what was underneath it all, because I was
too scared to look.

Dear Daughter:

      Instead of holding your hand I held tight
      to my vices
I waited for something, for someone else.
Took everything in your wake of leaving—the
drink, the money, the infidelity.
I didn't know what I had—

      you, what I believed to be a thorn in my

      garden, piercing me to get my attention,
to remind me that you are perfect, not just the
idea
of what I wanted you to be.

# Warmth

Dear Daughter,
*There* you are!

> My dream, in my arms like a sleeping
> sun.

I could not wish for anything more than this
moment—you, your tiny, soft head, resting
on me.

> No matter what size you are, I'll never
not know what that sweet indentation is in my
breast—

Knowing your head was there, your ear hearing
my heart beating just for you. Oh, I love you.

Dear Daughter,

Remember—you remember, don't you?

> That time when—yes, oh, how much we
> laughed. The look in your eyes—*their*
> eyes!

And that moment, where—yes, exactly. You tell
the story so well. I will bring it up every time we
are in a group.

Whenever I feel blue, I think about the words
you said, the gifts you gave me, no matter how
homemade or grand. Your gestures, they kept
me going—the notes, the flowers. The simple
acts of service that, even if I scolded you for
doing it wrong, were always appreciated.

Oh, Daughter, the laughter we shared—even
during some of the darkest moments—were the
vines I needed to pull myself back up through
the brush. I often long for and lean on that
laughter we shared, the laughter we share.

Dear Daughter,
     Soft pops of champagne,
a cheese board and
small plates—
     simple luxuries—
I always looked forward to when you came
home.

Catching up over the kitchen counter, I tell you
to stop when you try to help with the pasta.
     But you find a way, anyway, to assist.

Between your latest date
     and recent promotion, your current
adversities—I just sigh,
          I listen and watch your eyes, lit up
          like fireflies.
Your voice carries through this house—echoes
of the past fill me while you speak about the
world, all at your fingertips.
You navigate it with grace
and curiosity.

I listen, setting up the table,
   we pick and eat and laugh.

These are luxuries.

Dear Daughter—
Your hand was so small when we walked those
shores.

Your fingers clung to me, but you drifted to
pick out your next-favorite shell.
       I love how you preferred the ones that
       were chipped—
you were drawn to their obscurity, the
asymmetric ways
they told their stories.

       Your hair was wild
and tangled—like dancing seaweed.
Music was your laughter and the seagulls you
chased after,
       the beat of your bare feet, padding the
       sand by lapping waters.

When the light just settled, you let out your last
cry of amusement,
then asked me to hold you.
I always did.

I always will.

Dear Daughter,

      Each season led us on a new walk on our
      neighborhood path.

When school began, sunlight glistened on the
creek and through your hair, tempered but still
young.


Anxious, you feared the unknown—looking
around at the ashes of summer, clinging onto
that

      Childhood freedom that,

you'd later learn, wasn't all that freedom had to
offer.


      In October, you felt bittersweet about
being too old to trick-or-treat—yet too young to
watch horror movies alone.

Auburn leaves crunched under your growing
feet—strong now, ready to run.

I wanted to hold your hand as the breeze
quickened with chill,

      but I had to respect that you needed
      space now, to grow.

I wasn't about to take this time with you for
granted, risk pushing your boundaries—I had
tried and failed, and learned from that already.

When I refused to go out in winter, you told
me—"Embrace it."
          So we did.
Hands holding hot chocolate, snow-colored
froth on our lips,
icy breaths visible as we talked about your
friends, your crush. I would knit you a new scarf
for
          Christmas—
The colors of the college you chose to go to.


          Spring always came so late, and so soon.
But the moment the sun stretched its arms, so
did we, and we remembered all the beauty that
would come after
          harsh darkness.

Thank you, my darling,
　　　for waking my bones, inspiring me to
move and keep my heart strong.
　　　On days where work weighed heavily, I
　　　was glad
to be nudged toward the door, and
　　　enjoy nature　　　with you.

Dear daughter,
        don't fret
—these thunderstorms are violent and *angry*,
but not at you.

rain, wind—this Earth always has something to
say.

you've been crying lately—a mother knows.
        let out what you
need to, your Mother and Nature
        will do the rest.

cling to me—
        your stuffed animal
                —your pet
                        —your pillow.
cling to what you need.

these storms are scary—but if you listen, they
will tell you something.
        what do you hear?

❖

Dear Daughter,

> No, we don't share the same blood. But
> the best love is the kind we choose,
> isn't it?

Yes, there were times when I worried—*will she
like me? Will she accept this nipple, this pacifier, this
life that is no longer mine but yours, all yours.*

> And still you saw me whole and raw and
> new because what came before you

wove into me, trees intermingling under the
same sun.

Daughter, I found you, treasure, priceless.
Daughter, always my daughter.

Dear Daughter,

Recall the honeysuckle moments where we pressed our faces against the flowers on the Earth.

We cloud-watched and imagined. You reminded me of what it was to be a Daughter again.

Dear Daughter,
     I will follow your lead
         For what you need.
Heartbreak is an illness that can be cured with
the right medicine.
     I'm no doctor, but I am your mother,
And mothers know.

If you'd like, I will hold you as you cry and settle
into a hug on that old couch.

Oh, I could go on—about how they weren't
right for you,
     How my angel deserves the world,
If you want me to, I will.

I would literally—
     no, not figuratively,
         Kill for you.

Instincts *scream,* and there are times when I see
you hurt like this, that I would wring
their fragile throats
        because they don't know what happens
        when a Mother has been provoked.

Dear Daughter,

You never did care, did you, that we had nothing?

I tried

my best

for you, I always did—

but we didn't get the most lavish things life had to offer.

Still, you never judged me—in fact, you loved me, for all the things that it taught you.

The way we shared precious moments, opening them up like thousands of gifts, unlocking something new and different and gentle.

Your dimples, your chuckle. Your hand grabbing mine, that wide-eyed look. Oh! To feel needed.

And now you know—the feeling, how incredible it is, to be needed in that way, in a sacred, cyclic, intrinsic way.

# Encouragement

Dear Daughter,
No amount of religion, prayer, quotes, or
blessings
>will ever quite cover the cost of pain
you've held.
>I know this now.
Our history runs like our veins, connected and
true to a past that intertwines within us.
Yes, I may have given you tortured moments,
sacrifice, fear—
>but this DNA isn't for the weak.

It belongs to you—a being who is strong when
they shouldn't have to be,
>your beautiful, commanding presence,
a bright mind that wonders and
questions and, to a fault, ruminates.
True, I am a part of you.
>But your agency is yours to use,
>>to decide, divide, and conquer,
what you do with your body, and what you
don't.

Dear Daughter,
What is beauty?

> The individual strands of hair on your
> head, the color of your skin?
> Is it the soft blush in your cheeks or the
> exact amount you weigh?
> Is it the perfectly defined makeup you've
> crafted to complete a look dictated by
> someone else?
> Is it the ribs that you can see?

Dearest daughter, beauty, your beauty, it
is      untouched. It is your brain, your
strength.
Mirrors screamed pointless words and you
heard them, ate them—and then you blamed
yourself, for being "fat."
Oh, dear—daughter, no. No—we are made of
the same biology, and how dare I criticize that?

Did you know? We can move like angels, we
are *capable*, we destroy mirrors and scales
and demand the world to see us—both our
similarities and differences.

Did you know? *Your mind* is beautiful.
    Your intelligence lights up the night sky
    while I read to you
    Synapses an orchestra in the songs you
    create and tell the world
I wish I told you better stories about myself,
because I'd know—you'd reflect them back.

Dear Daughter,
If you could hear me now, I'd be cursing.
        I would show you how okay it is to be
        mad and wild and free.
From up here, there's no fear—I send that
feeling down to you, to remember that your
soul
        is felt, even from so far away.

*Fuck* that pig who hurt my girl. And screw his
friends too, for trying to woo you.
To hell, that misogynistic bear of a boss who
grilled you. I may have worked too hard, but
that doesn't mean you should, too.

In fact, take the day off.

And while you're at it, get yourself a sundae,
        go to a matinee. Alone.

The power of being alone—
        you never knew me when I was single.
Lost in the jungle and chaos of what the world
screamed back at her.

You may not always be able to tell,
but your mother—she was a powerful woman,
and she made you.

Dear Daughter,

I never did tell you enough how proud I am of you.

Regret is too sorrowful—rather, I feel the emptiness you must have felt when I didn't say what I should have. I feel the weight of not knowing, because dear, I once was you.

No, my mother didn't tell me what I wanted to hear. But I promise to take the best parts of her and sprinkle them onto you, my fairy, my star,

And though I can't shield you from all of me, please, take what you want.

Conjure the best and the worst of us all,

keep making us proud by being raw, authentic you—keep breaking the ropes cast since you were born; the traps set by men, the messages yelling from within, the expectations that bleed out from every screen.

You are the hero of all of our stories.

Dear Daughter,

You're in the thick of it now. I'm here, watching
you on the bathroom floor, and you should
know, I did the same thing—

      I cried, pressed my head into the wall,
      used toilet paper for tissues.

We cast the same shadows, but take comfort
that this is not in vain—

We are human, untamed. Make mistakes.

      I may never be forgiven, and they might
      not forgive you. But you, you're the
      center here—

The sun in my world that has been turned
upside down and on its side.

I watch you from within the hourglass and
knock hard through the sand,

      Understand,

            You are, were, and never will be,
            alone.

Dear Daughter,

  Keep playing your music.

I may sit and doze, after all, I'm an older woman now,

But take it as a compliment.

  My own mother told me that quality music

    is the kind you can peacefully
      fall

        asleep  to.


Continue painting, my love.

  Yes, everyone has access to color, but your dance of it is what makes you shine.


Work hard, dear—not because you must, but because you want to. I see how the tough days

  leave you feeling satisfied with a hint of

Magic in your eyes.

Dear Daughter,

      Bittersweet *is* the best flavor.

I know today is golden, celebratory. And I know
that comes with a price of missing those of us
who could not attend,

      tend to,

            watch and listen,

As you glisten and laugh and dance and cry on
a day that makes us all want to hug each other.
I am here, dear daughter,

      Oh, dear daughter.

I'm right here.

Dear Daughter,

It's hard not to see the ways you've
encompassed me,
Selflessly sharing the parts of me that weren't
quite damaged. And if they were, you shined
them, presented them anew. You are a gift.

It was never your job, but it was appreciated—
the way you held your chin up when I'd always
looked down. And now, seeing you stand with
grace and understanding, I can say that my
strength is restored;

No ailment, illness, sickness could suck
me away from you now. And though we're more
than hugs apart,

I know you, dear girl—smart, willing,
determined. You will take the best parts of us,
and shed light onto the world.

# About the Author

A linguistics scholar and mental health advocate, Samantha Mineroff has been writing creatively since she first held a pencil. Her novella was nationally recognized by Scholastic during the 2013 Scholastic Art and Writing Awards. She became a passionate academic, winning the 2018 Best Seminar Paper Award for her paper "The Rhetoric of Major Depressive Disorder: Performativity and Intra-activity of Emotions in Major Depression." She was a recipient of the Viola Marple Scholarship and the *Daedalus* Poetry Award, and coauthored the paper, "Interpersonal touch and the achievement of shared understanding in English conversation," which was presented at The Language and Social Interaction Working Group conference at Teachers College, Columbia.

Photo taken by Bryan MacNeill of Son Of Neill Aesthetics
Instagram: @sonofneill_aesthetics

After graduating from West Chester University with an English degree and dual minors in creative writing and linguistics, her professional writing grew and was featured on numerous mental health platforms, including *MedCentral*. In 2019, she presented her research on negative accommodation theory at the University of Liverpool during the Poetics and Linguistics Association conference. At just twenty-three years old, she was of the youngest to present.

When she isn't writing or researching, you'll find her listening to live music, singing and strumming a guitar, strolling through parks, and traveling the globe.